D0099240

RUNNING
WITH THE
GIANTS

JOHN C. MAXWELL

RUNNING WITH THE GIANTS

What Old Testament Heroes Want You to Know about Life and Leadership

Warner Faith

WARNER BOOKS

An AOL Time Warner Company

The author is represented by Yates & Yates, LLP, Literary Agent, Orange, California.

An AOL Time Warner Company

Book design by Fearn Cutler de Vicq
Printed in the United States of America
First Warner Books printing: September 2002
10 9 8 7 6 5 4 3 2 1

Library of Congress Cataloging-in-Publication Data

Maxwell, John C.
Running with the giants : what Old Testament heroes want you to know about life and leadership / John C. Maxwell.
p. cm.
ISBN 0-446-53069-7
1. Leadership—Religious aspects—Christianity. 2. Bible. O.T.—Biography. I. Title.

BV4597.53.L43 M295 2002
221.9'22—dc21 2002016848

As I continue to run my race, I dedicate this book to the following people. They ran life's race successfully and greatly influenced my life:

Grandpa Maxwell

Grandma Roe

Jim Butts

Pop Butcher

Glenn Leatherwood

Raymond Moats

Lon Woodrum

Bob Swisher

and

Clayton Porter, my father-in-law, who loved his God and his family. The lessons he taught were reflected in the life that he lived. His legacy lives in our hearts.

They are now in the crowd,
and I know they are cheering me on!

Contents

Acknowledgments

I'd like to say thank you to:
Charlie Wetzel, my writer
Kathie Wheat, my researcher
Linda Eggers, my assistant
Stephanie Wetzel, my proofer/editor
Rolf Zettersten, my publisher

A Cloud of Witnesses

On February 11, 2001, I had the privilege to speak at the NBA All-Star Game in Washington, D.C. My message that day centered on a favorite passage from Scripture:

> Since we are surrounded by so great a cloud of witnesses, let us lay aside every weight, and the sin which so easily ensnares us, and let us run with endurance the race that is set before us. (HEB. 12:1)

This verse is preceded by the Hall of Faith passage in Hebrews 11 that describes Old Testament giants: Abraham, Joseph, Moses, and Rahab, who ran life's course with great purpose and intensity. These verses have always been an inspiration to me because they portray an incredible picture. Can you see it? Just as professional basketball players, such as the ones at the NBA All-Star Game, are surrounded by cheering fans, you and I also have a great crowd of saints cheering us on as we run the race of life. The passage in Hebrews suggests that heaven is full of great men and women of faith who are rooting for our successful race through life.

I told the NBA All-Star players, coaches, and referees that it's our time to take the baton and continue the race that others have begun before us. Like the writer of Hebrews, we can receive inspiration, wisdom, and empowerment from those who have gone before us. We can see them in the stands and hear them cheering us on.

Do you wonder what those heroes of the faith

might be saying? When a crowd cheers, you can't distinguish one voice from another. But what if individuals could step out of the crowd, come down onto the track where you are running, and jog a lap with you? What would they say to you? Their time with you would be limited, so how could they share, in just a few words, the most important lesson they had learned from their own life? What words of wisdom would they use to encourage and empower you?

I shared that intriguing image at the All-Star chapel service. In my message, I offered words of inspiration that I believe some of the giants of the faith would share, were they to run a lap with us today. When I finished speaking, my friend Pat Williams, senior vice president of the Orlando Magic, said, "John, you should share these thoughts with more people by putting them in a book."

I have taken Pat's advice because I want you to be encouraged by the giants of the faith, just as I have been. What you will encounter on the following pages has grown out of my personal spiritual journey. Although I've studied Scripture for more than forty years, for the last two years I've focused particular attention on the lives of several biblical leaders—people whose faith influenced others and who continue to influence people today. While considering the life of each of them, I've continually asked myself, *If this person could step out of the crowd and come down onto the track to run with me, what would he or she say?*

I'd like you to join me in receiving the counsel I believe they would offer us. I think you will find that what these leaders of the faith have to say:

- is encouraging and empowering
- represents the essence of their lives
- is applicable to your life, and
- will elicit a "Yes!" response from you

We need what these men and women have to offer, because the race you and I are running is even more important than the NBA All-Star Game—or any other sporting event. Our race has an eternal impact. Together, you and I can run with the giants for a while to receive their inspiration, wisdom, and empowerment. We need that, because encouragement is the oxygen of the soul. Read slowly, breathe deeply, and run faithfully.

RUNNING
WITH THE
GIANTS

Noah

One Person Can Make a Difference

It's often said that life is a marathon. But I think it's much more challenging than that. When track athletes line up to run a marathon race, they know that a finish line awaits them exactly twenty-six miles and 385 yards ahead. For the very best runners, the finish comes in a little over two hours. They know before they start approximately how much time it will take to finish. And though they run most of the race on the open road, they often finish the course in a stadium of cheering fans.

The race of life is very different because you never know where the finish line is until you're actually crossing it. As I write this, I have been running my life-race for five and a half decades. I don't know where or when my race will come to an end, but I suspect that I am somewhere in the second half of it. You may be closer to the start, or you may be nearer to the end, but know that you are also in the race.

When I read that we are surrounded by "so great a cloud of witnesses" and that we should "run with endurance the race that is set before us" (Heb. 12:1), I picture myself running into a stadium filled with the giants of the faith. But unlike the Olympics, I'm not entering the stadium to *finish* the race. I am doing it mid-race to receive encouragement from the people of faith who are watching me run.

Join me. You and I can enter that stadium together. While we run for a while on the oval track, you and I can receive energy from the crowd. They will inspire us to run faster and with more confidence—not only in the stadium, but also back out on the open road. And that will serve to empower us and keep us running the race until our Creator tells us we're done.

As you and I enter the stadium and begin our first circuit of the track, we see an ancient man coming out of the stands to greet us. His face is weathered, his hands are boney, and there is a hobble in his gait. He is far older than any other human being we've ever seen. As you and I approach him, we are surprised to find that he manages to fall in step alongside us. He turns to us and says: "*One person can make a difference.*"

He continues, "I know because when God decided to destroy the earth with water, He made a covenant with me so that humankind might not perish" (Gen. 8:21).

We realize, of course, it's Noah. The Bible says he lived to be 950 years old. Quite an accomplishment. But that's nothing compared to the way he lived his life. His righteousness saved humanity from extinction. The book of Genesis explains the world's condition during Noah's time. It says:

> Then the LORD saw that the wickedness of man was great in the earth, and that every intent of the thoughts of his heart was only evil continually. And the LORD was sorry that He had made man on the earth, and He was grieved in His heart. So the LORD said, "I will destroy man whom I have created from the face of the earth, both man and beast, creeping thing and birds of the air, for I am sorry that I have made them." *But Noah found grace in the eyes of the LORD.* (6:5-8, emphasis added)

Making a Difference

As we run with Noah, he shares encouraging words that offer five ways we can make a difference. He says:

You Can Make a Difference for Your Family

Living a life of integrity and obedience to God always has the potential to positively impact others. We don't always see it while we're fighting the good fight, but it happens just the same.

Noah was selected by God to build the ark because of the way he lived. Fortunately, his obedience didn't benefit just him. It also saved his family. Genesis 7:1 says, "The Lord then said to Noah, 'Go into the ark, you and your whole family, because I have found you righteous in this generation'" (NIV). Those closest to you benefit most when you do what's right.

You Can Make a Difference for God's Creation

No one will ever again fulfill the special role Noah did, but you don't have to be a Noah to make an impact on your world. Each of us can make the place where we live better than it was when we found it. Think about how you can improve your little corner of the world.

You Can Make a Difference for Future Generations

Once a young man observed a man in his eighties planting an apple orchard. The old man lovingly and painstakingly prepared the soil, planted the tiny saplings, and watered them. After watching for a while, the young man said, "You don't expect to eat apples from those trees, do you?"

"No," the old man replied, "but somebody will."

Your actions can help those who come behind you. Because of God's covenant with Noah, we can be assured that we are safe from the worldwide destruction of a flood. Earth's inhabitants are still receiving the benefit that came from one man's life of righteousness. Likewise, you and I can also benefit future generations. When you serve people or influence them positively—and encourage them to pass along to others what they have received—you create a chain of impact that can outlive you.

You Can Make a Difference for God

Too often we fail to realize our importance to God. Scripture says, "For the eyes of the LORD run to and fro throughout the whole earth, to show Himself strong on behalf of those whose heart is loyal to Him" (2 Chron. 16:9). God is always looking for someone to stand in the gap for Him, and He desires to partner with people who love Him.

That was the case for Noah. God was discouraged with the people He had created. Yet Noah found favor in God's eyes and caused Him to save humanity. Because of his relationship with God, Noah changed the course of history.

You Can Make a Difference at Any Age

Some people want to put restrictions on themselves according to their talent, intelligence, or experience. Others worry about their age. But with God, one person can always make a difference, regardless of circumstances or situation. And age means nothing to Him. When Jesus fed the five thousand, a boy provided the loaves and fishes (John 6:1-13). And in the case of Noah, when it began to rain and he entered the ark, he was six hundred years old! You're never too old—or too young—to make a difference for God.

Noah's Words of Encouragement

As we finish the circuit of the track and approach the end of our time together, Noah hurriedly shares a few last nuggets of wisdom with us:

◆ *"Don't be afraid to stand out in a crowd.* I know what it means to stand alone. No one encouraged me to follow God, yet I stood for Him—even when everyone else in the world stood against me. Difference-makers are different. Don't let that bother you."

◆ *"Don't be afraid to do something for the first time.* It was strange to build a boat far from any sea or river that could float it. And it had never rained before, so nobody could even imagine a flood. But I was more concerned with obeying God than looking foolish. So I just kept building. Don't allow the words 'It's never been done' to prevent you from doing what God asks."

◆ *"When you see a rainbow, remember that one person can make a difference.* I had never seen a rainbow until *after* I followed through on what God asked of me. He placed the rainbow in the sky as a covenant to humanity that He would never again destroy the world with water. The next time you see a rainbow, think of God's promise to you: You can make a difference!"

Noah's Prayer for Us

Dear Lord,

Please help my fellow runners to understand the power of one. Speak to them about the unique task You call them to, and give them the will and the power to follow through so that they, too, can make a difference.

Amen

And with that, Noah slows his gait and bids us good-bye. We watch as he returns to his place in the stands, and then we notice that a woman is coming out to run with us.

Noah's Discussion Guide

And the LORD said, I will destroy man whom I have created from the face of the earth; both man, and beast, and the creeping thing, and the fowls of the air; for it repenteth me that I have made them. But Noah found grace in the eyes of the LORD. (GENESIS 6:7-8)

As Noah leaves to go back into the stands, we realize our time with him was too short. Our mind is flooded with questions we want to ask him. This discussion section gives us an opportunity to study Noah's message and reflect on what we have learned from him.

QUESTION FOR NOAH: How difficult was it to obey God and do something that seemed so foolish to others? ________________________________

____

____

QUESTION FOR PERSONAL REFLECTION: How do you explain your own obedience to God to those who do not understand? ______________________

____

____

QUESTION FOR NOAH: Did your family ever try to discourage you from building the ark? ________

____

____

QUESTION FOR PERSONAL REFLECTION: Name a time when you did the right thing but your family thought it was the wrong thing. How did you respond? ______________________________

____

____

QUESTION FOR NOAH: Was it hard to live a righteous life in such an evil environment? ________

____

____

QUESTION FOR PERSONAL REFLECTION: What helps you to do right when those around you are doing wrong? ______________________________

____

____

QUESTION FOR NOAH: How did you feel when it began to rain and you realized that God's word was true and He was using you to make a difference?

____

____

____

QUESTION FOR PERSONAL REFLECTION: Name a time when God really "came through" and fulfilled a promise He made to you. Name a time when God used you to make a difference. ________________

____

____

Question for Noah: What did you think every time you looked to the sky and saw a rainbow?

____

____

____

Question for Personal Reflection: Do you have tangible reminders of God's faithfulness to you? If so, what are they? ___________________________

____

____

Esther

God Has a Place for You

As the woman descends from the stadium stands, we can see that she is opulently dressed. Her clothes are vibrantly colored and appear to be made of the finest silk. She is wearing gold jewelry and a crown studded with precious gems. Her grace and bearing lead us to believe that she must be royalty.

Now that she is getting closer, we can see that she is a mature woman. And she is breathtakingly gorgeous. As she comes alongside us, she seems to glide as we move down the track. "I must tell you something very important," she says. "*God has a place for you.*" Her voice is gentle but strong and pleasing to the ear. We look into her eyes and she says simply, "I am Esther."

If ever there was someone with a strong sense of place and destiny, it is Esther. However, for many of her years, she did not realize that God had a special place for her to serve Him. "For much of my life," she says, "I felt out of place. My parents died when I was very young, and I was adopted by my uncle Mordecai. There were times I felt out of place in his home. As I grew up in a strange country with different customs, again I felt out of place. And being a simple girl, being brought to the king's court made me feel out of place as well."

Esther lived during a time when the Hebrews had been taken from their homeland and exiled to Persia. She suffered many hardships in her life, but she also received a rare opportunity. When King Ahasuerus of Persia sought a new queen, all the most beautiful young, unmarried women in the land were brought together and prepared to be presented to him. That included Esther, even though she was Jewish—a fact she did not share with others. To her delight and that of Mordecai, she was chosen by Ahasuerus to be the queen.

It looked as if Esther's life was destined for a happy, storybook ending. But then an official named Haman in the king's court plotted to have all the Jews in the entire kingdom executed—simply because of a grudge he held against Mordecai. When Mordecai discovered the plan, he sought Esther's help. To save their people, Mordecai wanted her to appeal to the king.

Finding Her Place

Have there been times when you felt you weren't where you belonged? People often feel that way. Sometimes we lack close relationships with others. Other times we question our ability to do the job required of us. We simply feel out of place. We fear that we will never feel at home. Esther understands. All her life she felt out of place, having been dislocated from her family, culture, and country.

But she encourages us with these words: *"No place is out of place when you're in God's place."* Then she continues her story.

Mordecai's request of her was no small one. For Esther to try to make a difference for her people, she would need great courage. At the time, if anyone who had not been summoned by the king appeared before him—and he wasn't pleased—that person would be executed! For thirty days Esther had not been called to go before the king. If she went to him on her own, she would be risking her life. Because she did not yet understand that God had uniquely placed her where He wanted her in order to accomplish His will, she at first refused. Scripture says,

> And Mordecai told them to answer Esther: "Do not think in your heart that you will escape in the king's palace any more than all the other Jews. For if you remain completely silent at this time, relief and deliverance will arise for the Jews from another place, but you and your father's house will perish. *Yet who knows whether you have come to the kingdom for such a time as this?"* (ESTHER 4:13-14, emphasis added)

Mordecai's words changed the way Esther felt about herself. For the first time, she realized that God had a place for her. Her hesitation was replaced with direction. Her questions were dissolved with newfound convictions. She was ready to take action. Scripture describes her immediate response:

> Then Esther told them to reply to Mordecai: "Go, gather all the Jews who are present in Shushan, and fast for me; neither eat nor drink for three days, night or day. My maids and I will fast likewise. And so I will go to the king, which is against the law; *and if I perish, I perish!*" (ESTHER 4:15-16, emphasis added)

Esther came to realize that her privileges were not just for her pleasure. She had been put in the palace for a purpose.

Courage and initiative come when you understand your purpose in life. What Esther experienced brings to mind the words of Winston Churchill: "In every age there comes a time when a leader must come forward to meet the needs of the hour. Therefore, there is no potential leader who does not have an opportunity to make a positive difference in society. Tragically, there are times when a leader does not rise to the hour." God not only has a place for us; He has placed us where He needs us. The decision is ours as to whether we will do what we can where we are.

Esther's Words of Encouragement

Esther's story itself is a great encouragement to us. It is reassuring to remember that God is always with us and to know that we can be used by God no matter where we find ourselves. But Esther isn't done. As we make the final turn on the track, she tells us this:

- *"For a period of time, you may not understand God's planning and purpose for your life.* That was certainly true for me. If you are in a season of life where you don't yet understand God's plan, take heart. Just because you don't comprehend God's plan for your life doesn't mean He doesn't care or doesn't have one. Have faith and remain obedient to Him."

◆ *"When you realize God's purpose for your life, you feel empowered.* When Mordecai explained to me that God might have made me queen just to save His people, my heart soared within me! And it steeled my resolve. When the time comes that you recognize a call of God on your life, it will fire you to action—even in the face of opposition or danger."

◆ *"Taking a risk is easier when you know God is in control.* When I said to Mordecai, 'If I perish, I perish,' I wasn't being fatalistic. I was placing myself in God's hands, knowing that even death is something that can be faced with confidence when you trust God. Not only does God have a place for us here on earth, He also has one prepared for us in heaven."

Esther's Prayer for Us

Heavenly Father,

Allow my friends to look beyond adversity or feelings of insecurity to see Your greater purpose. Empower them to take joy in the place where You have put them, take comfort in the knowledge that You are in charge, and take action to fulfill the purpose for which You have called them.

Amen

When Esther is done praying for us, she glides back toward the stands to take her place with the others.

Esther's Discussion Guide

So it came to pass, when the king's commandment and his decree was heard, and when many maidens were gathered together unto Shushan the palace, to the custody of Hegai, that Esther was brought also unto the king's house. (ESTHER 2:8)

As Esther leaves to go back into the stands, we realize our time with her was too short. Our mind is flooded with questions we want to ask her. This discussion section gives us an opportunity to study Esther's message and reflect on what we have learned from her.

QUESTION FOR ESTHER: How did you feel the times that you felt "out of place?" ______________________

____

____

QUESTION FOR PERSONAL REFLECTION: How do you feel and respond when you leave your comfort zone and feel out of place? ______________

____

____

QUESTION FOR ESTHER: Were you surprised by your sudden success and how did you respond? ______

____

____

QUESTION FOR REFLECTION: When success is sudden and change inevitable, how do you respond? ____

____

____

QUESTION FOR ESTHER: Would you have known God's will for your life without the problems that occurred? ______________________

____

____

QUESTION FOR PERSONAL REFLECTION: How has God revealed His will for you? Through others like Mordecai? Through difficult times? ___________

____

____

QUESTION FOR ESTHER: Why did you ask others to pray for you before you went to the king? ______

____

____

QUESTION FOR PERSONAL REFLECTION: Do you pray before you take action? Do you seek prayer support from others? How does this help you? ____

____

____

QUESTION FOR ESTHER: When should we, like you, take a risk for God and others? ___________

____

____

QUESTION FOR PERSONAL REFLECTION: Name a time when you took a risk for God and others. Would you do it again? ______________________________

____

____

Joseph
Don't Give Up on Your Dreams

At Esther's disappearance back into the stands, a man steps out and approaches the track. He is wearing white robes and, surprisingly, an Egyptian headdress. The first person you might think of is Pharaoh, the man who oppressed the Hebrews and opposed Moses prior to the Exodus. But he was not a person of faith, and you know he would not be in the stadium among the believers present to encourage us. Then it hits you. This is Joseph, the son of Jacob, who went from privileged son to the pit of slavery to the palaces of Egypt.

As he strides up to us, he immediately begins speaking. He says, "Dreams are conceived long before they are achieved. The period of time between the birth of a dream and its realization is always a process. This period is filled with doubts, adversity, changes, and surprises. During the process, you will experience good days and bad days. And frequently you will be faced with a dilemma: Do you give up, or go on? Without hesitation, I can give you the answer: *Don't give up on your dream.*"

Taking the Dream All the Way

As we begin our way around the track, Joseph wastes no time in imparting wisdom learned from a life of adversity. He tells us:

Don't Give Up on Your Dream Even If You Didn't Start Off Well

Joseph's dream came to him early—when he was seventeen years old. That's when he received visions from God that one day his brothers and even his father would bow down to him. Joseph immediately shared that information with his family, and it got him into trouble. But it didn't stop him.

The beginning of a dream often generates more enthusiasm than wisdom. We say things we shouldn't say and do things we shouldn't do. Like Joseph, we sometimes do not start off well. But, unlike Joseph, too often we give up on our dreams in the early stages when they are most fragile. Joseph encourages us to recapture the dream we abandoned and once again claim it as our own.

Don't Give Up on Your Dream Even If Your Family Doesn't Support It

The Bible says that when Joseph told his family about his dream, his father responded, "What is this dream that you have dreamed? Shall your mother and I and your brothers indeed come to bow down to the earth before you?" (Gen. 37:10). His brothers' response was worse:

> Then they said to one another, "Look, this dreamer is coming! Come therefore, let us now

> kill him and cast him into some pit; and we shall say, 'Some wild beast has devoured him.' We shall see what will become of his dreams!" (GEN. 37:19-20)

Clearly, Joseph wasn't going to get any support from anyone in his family.

It is very difficult to retain your dream when your family wants you to release it. But when your dream comes from God, the dream holds you when you feel unable to hold it.

Don't Give Up on Your Dream Even If Your Journey Is Full of Surprises

Just because things don't go as planned, that's no reason to give up. Look at the surprises Joseph lived through and how he reacted:

Misunderstood by his family	Give up?
Sold into slavery by his brothers	Give up?
Living in a strange country far from home	Give up?
Given favor in Potiphar's house	Go on!
Wrongly accused by Potiphar's wife	Give up?
Thrown into prison	Give up?
Put in charge of all the prisoners	Go on!

Forgotten by the chief butler	Give up?
Remained in prison two years	Give up?
Interpreted Pharaoh's dream	Go on!
Became second in command of Egypt	Go on!

Why didn't Joseph give up? After all, like you and me, he had twice as many *give-ups* as *go-ons.* Every dream contains negative surprises that can greatly discourage you. How did Joseph have the strength not to give up on his dream? Every time he found himself in a give-up time of life, he realized that the Lord was with him. That's what mattered. As the saying goes:

> God is too good to be unkind.
> God is too wise to be confused.
> When I cannot trace His hand,
> I can always trust His heart.

Even when life made no sense to Joseph, it made sense to God.

Don't Give Up on Your Dream Even If It Takes a Long Time to Realize It

Twenty-three years passed from the time Joseph had the dream until it was fulfilled. But in the end, Joseph ruled his family, was reconciled with his brothers, and saved the nation of Israel. You never know what God's timetable will look like. When you're in the middle of the journey, never give up on your dream.

Joseph's Words of Encouragement

Joseph has so much to say and so little time to share it with us. As we come nearer to the end of our lap, he says:

- "*God is always with you.* It's especially important to remember that during the toughest times. When I was lying in the pit, I didn't give up hope because I knew God was watching over me. (He *did* keep my brothers from killing me!) And when I was tempted by Potiphar's wife, I also knew God was there with me. Remember, my friends, in trials and temptation, God is with you too."
- "*Develop yourself during the down times.* When you suffer injustice or hard times, complaining doesn't do you any good. When people knock you down, the best thing you can do is allow

it to make you better. Each time I found myself in trouble, I tried to learn something new. You must try to do the same."

◆ *"Realize that self-promotion can never replace divine promotion.* Every time I tried to promote myself, it worked against me. Look what happened when I told my brothers about my dream! By the time I was presented to Pharaoh, I had finally learned my lesson. I knew that my successes came from God—and I gave Him the credit. The only advancement that matters is the kind God gives."

◆ *"When the dream is realized, it is sweeter than you can ever imagine.* When the dream is God-given, its fulfillment is worth the wait. Do you know what it was like to finally be reconciled with my family and tell my brothers, 'You meant evil against me; but God meant it for good, in order to bring it about as it is this day, to save many people alive' (Gen. 50:20)? As a boy, I dreamed only of power for my own gain. But by God's grace, I was able to save my family, live on prime land, lead the most powerful government on earth, and help preserve God's people for His greater purpose. The realization of my dream far exceeded my expectations. God has in mind for us more than we can imagine. He is the giver of every good and perfect gift, and the fulfiller of every dream He gives."

Joseph's Prayer for Us

Sovereign Lord,

I don't ask that You relieve every pain experienced by my friends; I ask that You fuel them to fulfill their purpose. Make Your dream for their lives vivid in their minds, and give them the heart to keep running the race.

Amen

When Joseph finishes praying, he briefly grasps each of our shoulders and gives a quick squeeze of encouragement. Then he departs for the stands. And that's when we see the next giant of the faith coming down to greet us. It's a man with a long beard carrying a staff in his hand. Immediately, my intuition tells me it must be Moses.

Joseph's Discussion Guide

> *Now Israel loved Joseph more than all his children, because he was the son of his old age: and he made him a coat of many colours. And when his brethren saw that their father loved him more than all his brethren, they hated him.* (GENESIS 37:3-4)

As Joseph leaves to go back into the stands, we realize our time with him was too short. Our mind is flooded with questions we want to ask him. This discussion section gives us an opportunity to study Joseph's message and reflect on what we have learned from him.

QUESTION FOR JOSEPH: Was it frustrating to have a dream and not have your family support it?

____

____

____

QUESTION FOR REFLECTION: Have you shared a dream with your family that they did not understand? What was it and how did you feel? ______

____

____

QUESTION FOR JOSEPH: When things went wrong, how tempted were you to give up? ____________

____

____

QUESTION FOR REFLECTION: Do you quit easily when things go wrong or when you don't understand what is happening to you? ______________

____

____

QUESTION FOR JOSEPH: How did you know that the Lord was with you during these difficult times?

____

____

____

QUESTION FOR REFLECTION: How do you know that the Lord is with you during difficult times? Do you sometimes forget? If so, why? ____________

____

____

QUESTION FOR JOSEPH: How difficult was it to forgive your brothers? ____________________

____

____

QUESTION FOR REFLECTION: How difficult is it for you to forgive others who have wronged you? Are there people you haven't forgiven? If so, what can you learn from Joseph that will help you forgive them? ________________________________

____

____

QUESTION FOR JOSEPH: Did you only see the hand of God on your life after you realized your dream?

___

___

___

QUESTION FOR REFLECTION: Do you see God's hand upon your life at all times, or just during the good times? What needs to happen in your life that will allow you to sense God's favor during uncomfortable situations? ___

___

___

Moses

Live in the Faith Zone, Not the Safe Zone

As Moses approaches us, I can't wait for our time with him. There is so much to admire about his life. I wonder what we will talk about. Will it be the creativity his mother used when placing him in a basket in the Nile to save his life when he was a baby? Will we learn about his burning-bush encounter with God? Or the parting of the Red Sea? Or how he received the Ten Commandments? Better yet— perhaps he will give us leadership insights, such as how he managed to lead two million constantly complaining people! There are so many things he could teach you and me!

Soon we are running our lap together. For a while, we simply travel side by side, waiting to hear what he says. Finally Moses, the man who spoke with God face-to-face as one would to a friend, says, "*Live in the faith zone, not the safe zone.*"

Stepping Out in Faith

As we continue running, Moses seems to consider what he wants to tell us. Finally he says, "Each person's life story is written in risks—the ones taken and the ones avoided. Look at my life. Do you think you would know my story if I hadn't stepped out of the safe zone? Would I even be talking to you right now if I hadn't entered the faith zone?" His gaze is fixed on us. It is intense.

"The greatest moment in my walk with God came at the burning bush," Moses continues. "The decision I made there that day wrote the next forty years of my life story. It is a decision that brought daily encounters with the living God! But in the moment of decision, it was not easy to make."

Moses goes on to describe what he had to overcome in order to move out of the safe zone and into the faith zone:

Moses Overcame the Experiences of His Past

Moses was born into uncertainty, but after his mother put him into God's hands and he was taken in by Pharaoh's daughter, he lived a life of comfort. He grew up in the safe zone—the palace of the king of Egypt, and he wanted for nothing.

Then, when he was forty, he took a risk. He left the safe zone and tried to do something big on his own for his people. He killed an Egyptian while defending a fellow Hebrew. What was the result of his own human effort? Pharaoh wanted to kill him for it, and Moses had to flee everything he'd ever known.

For the next forty years of exile in the desert, Moses never forgot his experiences in Egypt. He became like the cat who once sits on a hot stove and is determined never to get on a stove again. Moses felt he had learned his lesson: Egypt was not the place for him!

Moses Overcame the Comforts of His Present

Sad is the day when a person becomes absolutely satisfied with the life he is living, the thoughts he is thinking, the deeds he is doing—when there forever ceases to beat at the door of his soul a desire to do something greater for God.

After Moses left Egypt, he spent the next forty years in the wilderness of Midian tending sheep. He grew accustomed to the lifestyle there. The desert became another safe zone for Moses. Jethro took him in and made him part of his family. Moses took one of Jethro's daughters as his wife and they had a son. Moses had a secure place in the family business. Since Jethro had no sons of his own (only daughters) Moses became the heir apparent. Why would he want to leave all that? He had forged a new life for himself, and while it wasn't in a palace, it was very comfortable. He had left Egypt behind forever and made a complete transition. Or at least that's what he thought.

Moses Overcame the Insecurity of His Future

When God called Moses through the burning bush and told him to leave his comfortable situation and go back to Egypt to accomplish his life's mission, Moses felt totally unqualified to lead. He was insecure about himself and his future. As a result, he had many questions and doubts:

- "Who am I that I should go?" (Ex. 3:11)
- "What shall I say to them?" (Ex. 3:13)
- "But suppose they will not believe me?" (Ex. 4:1)
- "But I am slow of speech." (Ex. 4:10)

Every time Moses raised an objection to God's call, God answered it thoroughly. But Moses was still afraid. "O Lord," he finally cried, "please send someone else to do it" (Ex. 4:13 NIV). Fortunately for Moses, God wouldn't take no for an answer. And though afraid, Moses finally did the only thing that helps when we are uncertain about our future: He leaned on God, the One who knows our future in every detail. In doing that, he agreed to answer God's call, leave his comfort zone, and return to Egypt. As a result, the Children of Israel were delivered out of the hands of Pharaoh.

Moses' Words of Encouragement

We can see that our time with Moses is coming to a close, and before we part, he shares with us these truths:

- "*We do not naturally leave the safe zone.* I didn't want to leave Egypt; it was all I knew. Yet if I hadn't, I never would have experienced the burning bush. Then I didn't want to leave the Midian desert. But if I hadn't left the desert, I never would have seen God part the Red Sea or deliver His people. And I never would have talked to God face-to-face. Just because you don't want to do something doesn't mean you shouldn't!"
- "*Growth begins when we leave the safe zone.* For forty years, I benefited from everything Egypt had to offer. But only after I left Egypt for the first time did I begin to learn what was really important. And it took another forty years in the desert

to discover how God intended to use me. By then, I had been broken and remade by God. I had learned humility. You can't stay the same and learn at the same time. If you want to grow, you need to go."

◆ *"The safe zones rob us of our greatest moments and memories.* Many people are so afraid of risk that they spend their entire lives in Egypt, the land of 'not enough.' A few are willing to get out of their safe zone, and as a result, they enter the desert, the land of 'just enough.' But God wants more for you. He wants you to leave the wilderness and enter the promised land, the land of 'more than enough.' It was by faith that I left my comfort zone, and that is what is required of you if you want to enjoy God's blessings to the fullest. Twenty years from now, you will be more disappointed by the risks you *didn't* take than by the ones you *did.* Defeat tomorrow's regret by moving forward and getting into the faith zone today."

Moses' Prayer for Us

Lord God, the God of my fathers,

Give my friends a healthy discontent. Draw them out of the safe zone so that they may live every day in the faith zone. Make them wholly dependent on You, so that they can do things greater than themselves.

Amen

Moses' prayer is little more than a whisper, but there is incredible power in it. For a moment, all I can think of is, *We've talked with the man who spoke with God face-to face!* As soon as Moses finishes speaking, he is gone. You and I see his back retreating from us as another figure emerges from the stands.

Moses' Discussion Guide

And the daughter of Pharaoh came down to herself at the river; and her maidens walked along by the river's side; and when she saw the ark among the flags, she sent her maid to fetch it. And when she had opened it, she saw the child. (EXODUS 2:5-6)

As Moses leaves to go back into the stands, we realize our time with him was too short. Our mind is flooded with questions we want to ask him. This discussion section gives us an opportunity to study Moses' message and reflect on what we have learned from him.

QUESTION FOR MOSES: Did your mother ever tell you that God protected you for a reason? ______

____

____

Question for Personal Reflection: Can you point to a person or experience that gave you the feeling you were special and God had a plan for your life? If so, when or who? ________________

____

____

Question for Moses: Why did you feel inadequate when God asked you to deliver the Children of Israel? ______________________________

____

____

Question for Personal Reflection: List the reasons you feel inadequate when God asks you to do something. Are you letting those reasons keep you from obeying Him? ____________________

____

____

QUESTION FOR MOSES: The burning bush was a breakthrough in your life. How did that experience change you? ______________________________

____

____

QUESTION FOR PERSONAL REFLECTION: Have you experienced a spiritual breakthrough in your life? What was it? What did it do for you? __________

____

____

QUESTION FOR MOSES: Was it difficult going back to the place where you had previously failed and try the second time to deliver God's people? ______

____

____

QUESTION FOR PERSONAL REFLECTION: Is there a person or situation you have avoided because of a negative previous experience? What is it and what will you do about it? ______________________________

____

____

QUESTION FOR MOSES: Many times you were taken out of your comfort zone to obey God. Did it ever get easy? ______________________________

____

____

QUESTION FOR PERSONAL REFLECTION: Are you out of your comfort zone in any area because of your obedience to God? What is it and what are you learning? ______________________________

____

____

Rebekah

Give Generously to Others

We are still reflecting on Moses' words when we realize that a woman has emerged from the stands and is approaching us. Before we can even speculate who she is, she begins talking to us. She says, "Nothing seemed unusual to me that evening as I approached the town spring. While I awaited my turn to draw water, I visited with friends and talked about the day's events.

"After I drew the water," she continues, "I placed the jar on my shoulder and began the walk toward home. Then a stranger came up to me and asked for a drink. He was an older man with a kind voice. He was dressed like a servant, but obviously from a good house. And he was dusty, like he had been traveling a long time.

"Without hesitation, I lowered my jar and gave him some water. He took a good, long drink, and that's when I noticed his camels. As thirsty as he was, I realized that his camels must also be in need of water. So I offered to give them water too." She grabs each of us by the sleeve and says, "Little did I realize how this act of generosity would change my life and the lives of so many other people. Little did I know that my actions were the answer to a servant's prayer and the plan of my sovereign God. All I did was do what I felt I should. You must do the same: *Give generously to others.*"

God's Gracious Plan

The woman is none other than Rebekah. She didn't know that the man she served was the chief servant of Abraham. He had been sent to find a bride for Abraham's son, Isaac. Just before Rebekah arrived, as the servant stood by the well after his long journey, he had prayed:

> O LORD God of my master Abraham, please give me success this day, and show kindness to my master Abraham. Behold, here I stand by the well of water, and the daughters of the men of the city are coming out to draw water. Now let it be that the young woman to whom I say, "Please let down your pitcher that I may drink," and she says, "Drink, and I will also give your camels a drink"—let her be the one You have appointed for Your servant Isaac. *And by this I will know that You have shown kindness to my master."* (GEN. 24:12-15, emphasis added)

No doubt, the servant must have wondered how many young women he would have to ask for a drink before finding someone who would water his camels. That would be no small offer. It wouldn't be like giving a dog a drink. He had ten camels, each of which could drink twenty gallons of water. Take a look at this camel-watering calculation:

10 camels at 20 gallons each = 200 gallons
200 gallons drawn with a 5-gallon jar = 40 trips
40 trips at (a conservative) 3 minutes each = 2 hours

What seemed like a simple offer of kindness would have taken Rebekah two hours to fulfill!

The Rebekah Principle

Rebekah went the extra mile. Her generosity stands in stark contrast to the prevailing attitudes today. Rebekah seemed to be saying, *I'll do what you asked me to do, then I'm going to do something more.* In contrast, many people today seem to be thinking, *I'm going to do the least that is expected of me, and I'm going to try to get the most out of it.* Sadly, this underlying spirit has even crept into the lives and thoughts of many people of faith. Few individuals desire to do more than they must. Everywhere you look you see an attitude of minimum effort for maximum payment.

If we desire to be more like Rebekah, then we need to keep in mind that:

You Can't Be Generous and Legalistic at the Same Time

Rebekah did more than what was required or expected. Her generous spirit was unusual. You can contrast her actions with the legalistic Pharisees whose religion could be measured with a yardstick. But legalism always leaves people miserable. Legalists become either unbearably arrogant or incurably insecure. If we want to be like Rebekah, we can't keep score.

You Can't Walk the Second Mile Until You've Walked the First

It's easy for people to talk about the great and generous things they intend to do in the future. But if they're not being generous with what they have now, then it is unlikely that they will suddenly change in the future. Rebekah started her service by first doing what was asked. She gave the stranger a drink. Only when she had completed that task did she take care of the camels. Likewise, we need to start by giving now where we currently are—not somewhere over the rainbow or someday far in the future.

Extra Blessings Result from Extra Effort

How easy it would have been for Rebekah to lower her jar, give the stranger a drink, and continue on to her home. That would have been the convenient thing to do. Before she made the offer, she undoubtedly thought about the time, effort, and sacrifice that would be required for her act of generosity. Yet, she did it anyway. That set her apart from all the other women who had gathered at the spring that evening. And as a result, her life changed in ways she could not have imagined.

Rebekah's Words of Encouragement

Rebekah knows she has just a few moments more with us, and there is an increased urgency in her words. She seems to know that to encourage generosity in others is to go against the flow of human nature. But now, like then, she perseveres. She says:

◆ "*When we give generously, we receive more than we would ever think possible.* Jesus says, 'With the measure you use, it will be measured back to you' (Matt. 7:2). We set the standard of what we receive by what we give. I gave a little more than I was asked to give, but I received much more than I ever expected to receive: I became the great-grandmother of the Messiah! Give what you can. You have no idea what God desires to give you in return."

◆ "*When we give generously, our loved ones will be blessed.* When Abraham's servant revealed who he was, he brought out gold articles and rich garments and gave them to me. But he also gave precious things to my mother and brother. There is always an overflow from generosity that blesses those close to the giver."

◆ "*When we give, the impact of our generosity often outlives us.* In the moment of giving, you cannot imagine how your actions might impact the lives of others in the future. Imagine what the world would be like if . . .

Michelangelo had said, 'I don't do ceilings.'

Noah had said, 'I don't do boats.'

Moses had said, 'I don't do rivers.'

David had said, 'I don't do Goliaths.'

Mary had said, 'I don't do virgin births.'

John the Baptist had said, 'I don't do baptisms.'

Peter had said, 'I don't do Gentile discipleship.'

Paul had said, 'I don't do letters.'

Jesus had said, 'I don't do crosses!'

A lifestyle of generous giving will outlive you here on earth and in eternity."

Rebekah's Prayer for Us

Sovereign Lord,

I ask that you would give my friends the eyes to see opportunities in the everyday events of life, the hands to reach out and give more than is required or expected, and the heart to do so with motives that are pure and not self-seeking.

Amen

As we watch Rebekah depart and return to her place in the stands, we feel a prompting in our hearts. We want to be more like her. Privately, I determine to find more opportunities to give generously in the here and now. Then I see the next person coming out to meet us.

Rebekah's Discussion Guide

And it came to pass, before he had done speaking, that, behold, Rebekah came out, who was born to Bethuel, son of Milcah, the wife of Nahor, Abraham's brother, with her pitcher upon her shoulder . . . And she said, Drink, my lord: and she hasted, and let down her pitcher upon her hand, and gave him drink. (GENESIS 24:15, 18)

As Rebekah leaves to go back into the stands, we realize our time with her was too short. Our mind is flooded with questions we want to ask her. This discussion section gives us an opportunity to study Rebekah's message and reflect on what we have learned from her.

QUESTION FOR REBEKAH: When you saw the servant's camels, did you think twice before offering to draw water for them? ______________________

____

____

QUESTION FOR PERSONAL REFLECTION: Do you hesitate to give when the request will take a lot of time, energy or money? When have you hesitated and not given? When have you hesitated and given?

____

____

____

QUESTION FOR REBEKAH: Were there times while you were drawing water that you were tempted to quit? ____________________________________

____

____

QUESTION FOR PERSONAL REFLECTION: Have there been times when you did not fulfill your commitment? Why did you quit? ______________

____

____

QUESTION FOR REBEKAH: Did you ever think that you would receive something for your generosity?

____

____

____

QUESTION FOR PERSONAL REFLECTION: Do you often ask, "What will I receive" before you become generous with others? When did you give generously to someone or something without asking, "What is in it for me?" ______________________

____

____

QUESTION FOR REBEKAH: How did you feel when others were blessed because of your generosity?

___

___

___

QUESTION FOR PERSONAL REFLECTION: Have others benefited from your generosity? Who and when?

___

___

___

QUESTION FOR REBEKAH: Did you realize that you were a direct answer to someone's prayer? ___

___

___

QUESTION FOR PERSONAL REFLECTION: When have you been a direct answer to someone's prayers? How did you feel when you found out? ___

___

___

Abraham

God Always Does the Right Thing

The man now stepping out of the crowd reminds me a little of Noah, although he is not nearly as old. His clothing is similar to Noah's, but he appears to be very well-to-do. Before we even have time to observe more about him, he quickly comes alongside us and immediately states, "My name is Abraham."

I can hardly contain myself. Right beside us is the man the Hebrews call their father. The nation of Israel and the fulfillment of God's plan really begin with Abraham and his family. Abraham was a friend of God!

I wonder what this great man will say to you and me. We've run only a few steps when Abraham says with great assurance: *"God always does the right thing."*

Learning to Trust God's Character

Without hesitation, Abraham begins to teach us about God and His faithfulness. He explains that:

God Always Does the Right Thing,
Even If It Takes a Long Time

When much time passes between when God promises something and when He fulfills it, we often act like small children who can't wait for Christmas. We don't like waiting, and we fear that we've been forgotten.

It's easy to see why Abraham (whose name was Abram before God changed it) became impatient. When God sent him out of Ur of the Chaldeans, He promised him that he would possess the land of

Canaan, he would have many descendants, and his offspring would become a great nation. The fulfillment of that promise would bring him great joy. But after ten years, God still hadn't delivered on His promise. Take a look at what that decade held for Abraham:

- He left his family and country.
- God promised to bless him and his descendants.
- Abraham lived through a famine.
- He feared Pharaoh and lied to him.
- He experienced family conflict—he and Lot separated.
- When Lot was kidnapped, he pursued the kidnapper and fought to rescue him.
- He still had no son.

After ten years and many trials, Abraham wanted to know whether the deal was still on. The Scripture states:

> After these things the word of the LORD came to Abram in a vision, saying, "Do not be afraid,

> Abram. I am your shield, your exceedingly great reward." Then He brought him outside and said, "Look now toward heaven, and count the stars if you are able to number them . . . So shall your descendants be." And he believed in the LORD, and He accounted it to him for righteousness. (GEN. 15:1, 5-6)

Even after this reassurance from God, Abraham still didn't know what God was up to. In a moment of doubt, he and Sarah tried to take things into their own hands by producing a son through Sarah's maidservant. But God's ways—and His sense of time—are not like ours. Even though it may seem like a long time to us, God always does what is right, and He always comes through. Abraham wants us to remember that.

God Always Does the Right Thing,
Even If What He Says Seems Absurd

When God told Abraham and Sarah, "I will certainly return to you according to the time of life, and behold, Sarah your wife shall have a son,"

Sarah laughed and said, "After I have grown old, shall I have pleasure, my lord being old also?"(Gen. 18:10, 12). Though she soon denied that she had laughed, she had good reason to: She was eighty-nine years old! Can you imagine what it was like explaining her pregnancy to friends! And why did God wait so long to fulfill the promise?

The answer is that God wanted Abraham's total trust. And that comes only through testing. God fulfilled His promise. The next year Sarah bore Isaac—even though it seemed impossible. Our minds cannot conceive all the things God is capable of doing. The words of God to Abraham best sum up His ability: "Is anything too hard for the LORD?" (Gen. 18:14).

God Always Does the Right Thing, Even If We Question Him

"Have you ever questioned God?" Abraham asks us. "Have you ever wondered about His character?" Before we can answer, he continues, "I have. When the Lord told me He was going to destroy the city of Sodom, home of my nephew, Lot, it worried me. *How could He do such a thing!* I wondered."

Abraham went on to describe how he talked with God concerning Sodom. He boldly asked God, "Will you sweep away the righteous with the wicked?" (Gen. 18:23 NIV). Then he began negotiating, asking God to spare the city for fifty righteous people, then forty-five, then forty, thirty, twenty, right on down to ten. He just wouldn't let it go.

But God is righteous as well as right. He honored Abraham's request; He saved the few righteous people who lived in Sodom, and He destroyed the depraved city. In the end, Abraham provided the answer to his own questions when he observed, "Shall not the Judge of all the earth do right?" (Gen. 18:25). God is a righteous judge. Just as He preserved the innocent in Sodom, He will take care of you and me.

God Always Does the Right Thing, Even If We Do Not Understand

The greatest test of Abraham's trust came when

God asked him to sacrifice his beloved son, Isaac. Why would God want Abraham to kill his son of promise? It didn't make sense; it appeared to go against God's promise to make Abraham's descendants into a great nation.

By this time Abraham didn't question or doubt. He simply got up early the next morning to do what he had been asked. After many years of asking questions, negotiating with God, and reacting to God's direction, Abraham finally sought to be obedient. He had learned the secret of walking with God: Trust and obey. God had been faithful to every promise He had made, so Abraham trusted His character. He finally understood that we should not try to understand God until we have first obeyed Him.

Abraham's Words of Encouragement

Abraham speaks about God with an easy confidence, similar to the way a gray-haired saint who's been married for sixty or seventy years talks about a spouse. They've been through good times and bad together. They've faced tragedy and trials. They know—and trust—each other's character. Someday, we hope to be like him.

We are coming very close to the end of our lap with Abraham, and in the final moments, he shares two important truths with us:

- "*Perfection is not a prerequisite for God to begin His work in our lives.* I could hardly believe it when God called me to leave home and go to the land He would give my descendants. I went immediately, but I thought to myself, *Does He have the right person? What can God do with someone like me*? Even after I obeyed God's call, I still made many mistakes. You aren't perfect either, but that's not important. This is what matters: when you walk with God, your character becomes more like God's."
- "*God's blessings are never earned.* I did nothing to merit God's call upon my life. I didn't deserve the promise of the land or my many descendants or the grace and favor of God. They were all gifts. That became crystal clear when God asked

me to sacrifice Isaac and I laid him on the altar in obedience. God gave me everything, and He was free to take it away. As you know, God did not require me to take Isaac's life. It was a test of my gratitude and faith. Likewise, your life is a gift. Treat it that way. Be grateful, and no matter what happens, always trust God."

Abraham's Prayer for Us

Lord,

I ask that You help my friends have patience when it seems like a long time since they have heard from You. Help them . . .

to be obedient when your leading seems so strange,

to ask questions when they do not understand,

to trust you when they do not find answers,

because, God, You always do the right thing.

Amen

As Abraham leaves us, I am struck by how ordinary he is. And even that drives the point home to me: When we trust God, He can make the ordinary extraordinary! I meditate on that thought for a moment. Then I see someone else emerge from the stands and approach us.

Abraham's Discussion Guide

And they came to the place which God had told him of; and Abraham built an altar there, and laid the wood in order, and bound Isaac his son, and laid him on the altar upon the wood. And Abraham stretched forth his hand, and took the knife to slay his son. (GENESIS 22:9-10)

As Abraham leaves to go back into the stands, we realize our time with him was too short. Our mind is flooded with questions we want to ask him. This discussion section gives us an opportunity to study Abraham's message and reflect on what we have learned from him.

QUESTION FOR ABRAHAM: How could you have been called a "friend of God," and had all of your struggles? ________________________________

____

____

QUESTION FOR PERSONAL REFLECTION: In what areas do you struggle the most with God? Waiting on Him to fulfill His promises? Obeying Him when His way seems absurd? Questioning Him? Understanding Him? ________________________

____

____

QUESTION FOR ABRAHAM: Why did you so often try to provide a way when God did not wish to?

____

____

____

QUESTION FOR PERSONAL REFLECTION: What areas do you try to "fix" or "pull off" when God seems slow? ________________

____

____

QUESTION FOR ABRAHAM: Were you amazed at how far you negotiated with God about Lot's safety?

____

____

____

QUESTION FOR PERSONAL REFLECTION: Have you ever negotiated with God? How did it turn out?

____

____

____

QUESTION FOR ABRAHAM: How did you feel as a father when you placed Isaac on the altar? ________

____

____

QUESTION FOR PERSONAL REFLECTION: What is the most difficult thing in your life that you must surrender to God? Have you done it yet? ________

____

____

QUESTION FOR ABRAHAM: When you look back at all the blessings you received from God, how did you respond? ______________________________

____

____

QUESTION FOR PERSONAL REFLECTION: When you look at all of God's blessings on your life, how do you respond? List the responses. ____________

____

____

Nehemiah

No Problem Is Too Big When You Have Help

After running with so many giants of the faith and receiving their encouragement, I am feeling confident. What wisdom and perspective they have given us! Abraham's words on the goodness and grace of God make me feel like I'm ready for anything! I want us to leave the arena and once again resume our race—energized, prepared, and self-sufficient. I can't wait to act on the empowerment I have received, to put it to good use.

As I am considering asking you to turn toward the exit with me and leave the stadium, the next giant of the faith is already beside us. He looks like an official of some kind; he is wearing a gold chain around his neck indicating his official status, and he is carrying a small scroll.

The man looks at us, and he seems to sense my desire to go out and meet life head-on. He says, "There was a time in my life when everything was going well for me. I had access to the king daily, and I enjoyed the many pleasures of the palace. Mine was a coveted position, one that a foreigner doesn't usually achieve. You could say that I had 'arrived.'"

The man turns his head and looks you and then me in the eye. He says, "I am Nehemiah. I was cup-bearer to King Artaxerxes of Persia." Before we can react, he continues, "Then one day I received word about my hometown, Jerusalem. The walls of the city were in ruin and the gates had been burned to the ground. The people were unprotected from their many enemies. The news hit me like a blow. I began to weep uncontrollably. The situation was hopeless, and I was helpless to do anything about it. In my grief, I turned to God, and He made me understand something: *No problem is too big when you have help*. I knew what I had to do: ask the king for help."

Working Together

The rebuilding of the walls of Jerusalem is not the story of a single successful person. The walls were rebuilt because many people helped one another and worked together. First, Nehemiah sought the aid of his king, who agreed to send him to Jerusalem to rebuild the walls. When he got there, Nehemiah again asked for help. Scripture quotes his plea to the people:

> "You see the distress that we are in, how Jerusalem lies waste, and its gates are burned with fire. Come and let us build the wall of Jerusalem, that we may no longer be a reproach." And I told them of the hand of my God which had been good upon me, and also of the

> king's words that he had spoken to me. So they [the nobles, priests, and officials] said, "Let us rise up and build." Then they set their hands to this good work. (NEH. 2:17-18)

We enjoy hearing Nehemiah describe how the people banded together, family by family, and worked for a remarkable fifty-two days with swords in one hand and trowels in the other, rebuilding the wall.

When Should We Ask for Help?

With the wisdom of someone who has rallied a great group of people to do a work for God, Nehemiah shares with you and that:

We Should Ask Others for Help When the Problem Is Bigger Than Us

The problem Nehemiah faced was certainly bigger than he was. Look at what he was up against:

- Nehemiah was geographically far from the problem—more than one thousand miles away—when he learned of it.

- The people of Jerusalem had no materials to rebuild the walls.
- The people had no will of their own to take on the rebuilding project.
- There was great opposition to the rebuilding project from their neighboring enemies.

When you and I face problems that are bigger than us, it's not time to get discouraged; it's time to get help!

We Should Ask Others for Help When the Problem Becomes Personal

When Nehemiah heard about the state of Jerusalem, he mourned for many days. It wasn't just some bit of foreign news. It was personal. Max De Pree says, "The first responsibility of a leader is to define reality." As the leader for the rebuilding project, Nehemiah recognized the reality of the situation in the Judean capital, and it wasn't good!

We Should Ask Others for Help When We Have Shared the Problem with God

The first thing Nehemiah did when he heard about Jerusalem's condition was talk to God. Too often we try to carry the load of a problem all by ourselves. But the first person we should ask for help in any situation is God. The great hymn writer Joseph Scriven was correct when he penned the words:

> O what peace we often forfeit,
> O what needless pain we bear,
> All because we do not carry
> Everything to God in prayer!

Scripture asserts, "Let us therefore come boldly to the throne of grace, that we may obtain mercy and find grace to help in time of need" (Heb. 4:16).

We Should Ask Others for Help When We Are Willing to Do Our Part

God wants to be our partner throughout life. Too often we are tempted to either carry the entire load ourselves or give everything to God and do nothing. God doesn't like either strategy. Sometimes He moves before us and sometimes after us—but He doesn't move without us. Without God . . . we cannot. Without us . . . God will not. Just as Nehemiah was willing to go halfway across the known world to do what he could, so should you and I.

We Should Ask Others for Help When We Sense God's Approval for the Vision

When Nehemiah prayed, he asked God to give him favor. As Nehemiah obeyed God, he increasingly sensed that God had answered his request. Nehemiah says that when the king gave him permission to go back to Jerusalem and supplied him with letters and materials, "The king granted them to me according to the good hand of my God upon me" (Neh. 2:8). When Nehemiah stood before the people of Jerusalem to challenge them with the huge rebuilding project, he encouraged them by telling them of the "hand of my God which had been good upon me" (2:18). When opposition arose concerning the rebuilding of the wall, with confidence Nehemiah said, "The God of heaven Himself will prosper us; therefore we His servants will arise and build" (2:20).

Nehemiah's increased awareness of God's blessing was a direct result of his continued obedience.

"Never try to explain God until you've first obeyed Him," Nehemiah tells us.

We Should Ask Others for Help When People Oppose Us

Repeatedly Nehemiah and the people were confronted with opposition. When Nehemiah received permission and resources to go back to Jerusalem, the opposition was "deeply disturbed" (Neh. 2:9-10). When the people declared their intention to rebuild the wall, the opposition laughed at them and despised them (2:18-19). When the people actually began rebuilding the wall, the opposition became "furious and very indignant, and mocked the Jews" (4:1). When the people continued rebuilding the wall anyway, the opposition became very angry and conspired to attack them and create confusion (4:6-8). And finally, when the people finished rebuilding the wall, the opposition pretended to be reasonable, but they meant the people harm (6:1-9).

Motion always causes friction. But whenever God's people move forward, the enemy always increases its opposition, and that really turns up the heat. When others oppose us, it's not time to give up. It's time to get help.

Nehemiah's Words of Encouragement

As our time with Nehemiah comes to a close, I regret that you and I will not be able to run an additional lap with him. His leadership is incredible, and there is so much that I would like to learn from him. I listen eagerly as he shares these last thoughts with us:

- *"It isn't easy to ask for help.* I know. Even after I prayed and planned, I found it difficult to tell the king my heart's desire. Don't let insecurity or ego or fear make you try to go it alone. In God's kingdom, there are people ready to help you at the right time, in the right way—people you don't even know yet."
- *"Not everyone will help.* When I arrived in Jerusalem, I had momentum on my side. I had received permission and resources to rebuild. The leaders of the city had bought into my leadership

and vision. When we began rebuilding the wall, I thought, *Everyone is ready to work!* But to my surprise, some nobles did not put their shoulder to the work of the Lord. Remember this, no matter how great the vision, how strong the morale, or how far the progress, someone in your camp will refuse to help. Don't wait on them. Keep moving forward."

◆ "*Many times you don't need a miracle—you just need each other.* Many of the great men and women here in this stadium saw God provide for them miraculously. But you don't always need a miracle to do something miraculous! God had already provided all that we needed. We just needed to work together. Without the leadership I provided, the people would have remained fearful and inactive. Without the hard work the people provided, the walls would have remained in ruins. My friends, you *can* run this race well, but you *cannot* run it alone. Why do you think all of us are here encouraging you?"

Nehemiah's Prayer for Us

Sovereign King,
I ask you to give my friends . . .
courage to face their difficult problems,
faith to come to You before anyone else,
belief that others will come alongside to help them, and
favor with all whom they ask
because, God, no problem is too big when we have help.

Amen

As Nehemiah leaves, I look up into the stands and see thousands of individual faces smiling down on us. And I realize the foolishness of my wanting us to leave the arena early to run our own way. I have learned my lesson. I understand that I am not meant to run the race alone. And I gladly await my time to run with the remaining giants willing to come down to encourage and empower me. To my surprise, the next giant is a small girl who looks to be no more than twelve years old.

Nehemiah's Discussion Guide

And they said unto me, The remnant that are left of the captivity there in the province are in great affliction and reproach: the wall of Jerusalem also is broken down, and the gates thereof are burned with fire. And it came to pass, when I heard these words, that I sat down and wept, and mourned certain days, and fasted, and prayed before the God of heaven. (NEHEMIAH 1:3-4)

As Nehemiah leaves to go back into the stands, we realize our time with him was too short. Our mind is flooded with questions we want to ask him. This discussion section gives us an opportunity to study Nehemiah's message and reflect on what we have learned from him.

QUESTION FOR NEHEMIAH: When you heard the bad news about Jerusalem, how did you feel? ______

____

____

QUESTION FOR PERSONAL REFLECTION: When you hear bad news, do you respond like Nehemiah?

____

____

____

QUESTION FOR NEHEMIAH: Was it hard to ask for so many people to help you? ______________

____

____

QUESTION FOR PERSONAL REFLECTION: If you need help do you quickly ask for it? Who do you go to?

____

____

____

QUESTION FOR NEHEMIAH: Did you feel lonely or discouraged when you saw the destruction of the walls? ______________________________

____

____

QUESTION FOR PERSONAL REFLECTION: What makes you feel lonely? What discourages you? How are you strengthened? Reassured? Encouraged?

____

____

____

QUESTION FOR NEHEMIAH: The "hand of the Lord" upon you must have given you strength. Is that why you shared God's favor on your life with the people? ______________________________

____

____

QUESTION FOR PERSONAL REFLECTION: Do you share God's favor on your life with others? When was a time you felt the "hand of God" was upon you?

____

____

____

QUESTION FOR NEHEMIAH: How was the morale of the people after the wall was built? ______________

____

____

QUESTION FOR PERSONAL REFLECTION: What difficult task have you undertaken with others that brought glory to God and lifted your spirits? ____________

____

____

The Servant Girl

One Small Act Can Make a Big Difference

Who in the world could this child be? I wonder as the girl skips up to us and energetically takes her place running beside us. We have spent time with some of the greats of the faith, men and women who changed the world. We've run with Nehemiah, maybe the finest leader in the Bible, and with Abraham, father of the nation of Israel. Now we are paced by a little girl dressed in the humblest of clothing. Finally, I can contain myself no longer. "Who are you?" I ask.

Her answer is simple: "I am the servant of my mistress in the house of Naaman. You need to know: *One small act can make a big difference.*"

At once I remember. The Bible records only one statement this girl made. Her part in the Bible is so small that the Scripture writer doesn't even mention her name. The passage in 2 Kings says,

> Now Naaman, commander of the army of the king of Syria, was a great and honorable man in the eyes of his master, because by him the LORD had given victory to Syria. He was also a mighty man of valor, but a leper. And the Syrians had gone out on raids, and had brought back captive a young girl from the land of Israel. She waited on Naaman's wife. Then she said to her mistress, "If only my master were with the prophet who is in Samaria! For he would heal him of his leprosy." (5:1-3)

This little girl was a mere slave owned by Naaman, a powerful and highly respected man. Not only was he an outstanding general, the commander of the Syrian army and a trusted companion of the king, but he was also a great warrior. If there had been a "Who's Who" in Syria, his name would have been at the top of the list. There was only one stain on his résumé: He was a leper. For him to have achieved and maintained his position as military commander despite that affliction, he must have possessed unmatched skill.

"When I first came to the house of my master, Naaman, I was very unhappy," she says. "I had grown up in Samaria, the capital of Israel. Then I was forced into slavery in a strange house in a strange land . . . I just had to learn to make the best of it. Fortunately, my mistress was very nice, and she took good care of us.

"My master was different," she continues, "not unkind, but not warm either. I think his disease affected everything. In my country, he would have been an outcast. In his country, he could rise in rank, but people still rejected him. Maybe that's why he seemed happiest when he went to war, where he excelled. When he was home, he mostly kept to himself. And often he was very sick. All the servants worried about his health and took care of him.

"I wanted to help him too," she says, "but I felt

helpless. Then I got an idea. It didn't seem like much, and I wasn't sure if anyone would listen to me, but I decided to try anyway. I told them about the prophet Elisha. He was a true man of God, so I knew he had the power to heal my master."

One Small Act

The servant girl is speaking with complete confidence, as though what she did was an everyday matter. But it wasn't. She could have remained silent and safely anonymous, but instead she spoke up to Naaman's wife. It was really a remarkable act. Here is why:

She Acted Even Though She Was Small

Many times we discount what we can do because we think we are too small or powerless to make a difference. Consider this girl's situation:

- She was a slave, the lowest anyone could be in social standing.
- She was an outsider, a Jew living in Syria.
- She was young; why would a powerful leader listen to her?

- She was a female in a male-dominated culture.

By the standards of the day, she had *nothing* going for her—no power, no position, no possessions. The only thing she had was her faith—and that was enough. As God told the apostle Paul centuries later, "My grace is sufficient for you, for My strength is made perfect in weakness" (2 Cor. 12:9).

She Acted Even Though What She Could Do Was Small

As a member of the king's court, Naaman had access to the best physicians in the country. Everyone in his household undoubtedly watched as he tried every available treatment for his leprosy. Nothing worked. In the midst of all this activity, what the servant girl could do must have seemed rather small to her. After all, she couldn't heal Naaman, nor could she ease his pain. All she could do was make a suggestion to her mistress, yet she didn't let the seeming insignificance of that act stop her. Instead of being discouraged by what she couldn't do, she did what she could do.

She Acted Even Though the Stakes Were Not Small

The girl took a huge risk when she expressed her faith that God could heal Naaman. If he had gone to Israel to be healed and come back still sick—and looking foolish—he would no doubt have punished her. In fact, when he received permission from his king to leave Syria for Samaria, the stakes went up not only for the girl, but also for the entire nation of Israel. When Israel's king received Naaman and found out he expected to be healed, the king lost hope and tore his clothes in grief. He believed that the Syrian king was asking the impossible in order to start a war with his nation. But the prophet Elisha heard that Naaman had come. Elisha told the general what to do. And when Naaman obeyed Elisha's instructions to bathe in the Jordan River seven times, the Syrian commander was healed.

Scripture says that Naaman's skin was restored that day; it was like that of a child. More important, his faith also was changed. In that moment, he realized that God was God, and he sought to worship Him the rest of his life. One small person doing a small act made a big difference in his life.

The Servant Girl's Words of Encouragement

We are getting close to the stands now. In our last moments, she says,

- *"If you want to make a big difference, be confident.* My master listened to me because I believed in what I told him. We have a great God, and there is nothing He can't do. Live like you believe it."
- *"If you want to make a big difference, be credible.* I never would have had the courage to speak up if my service had not been pleasing to my master's wife. People always pay more attention to how you live than to what you say. Remember that when you desire to speak into the lives of others."
- *"If you want to make a big difference, speak to people's needs.* Everyone needs hope and help—even powerful people like my master. And if the individuals you desire to help are low on faith, lend them yours."

◆ *"If you want to make a big difference, don't be afraid to do something even if it seems small.* Only God knows how great an impact a small act can make."

The Servant Girl's Prayer for Us

God,

I ask that You give my friends understanding that no one is too small to make a big difference for You. courage to say and do the little things that can impact others' lives, and favor with the "big" people whose lives can be changed by small acts of kindness.

Amen

As she says good-bye, she adds, "I hope my time with you makes a difference. I know you will enjoy the next person you meet." Her voice softens and she says knowingly, "It's King David." Then she bolts back to the stands. That's when it becomes clear that one need not be a giant of a person to be a giant of the faith. I look in wonder at this girl who so easily put herself on the line by doing one small act for someone her countrymen would have dismissed and ignored. And I suddenly realize that we never got the chance to ask her name. I guess we'll never know it, but we do know this: One small act really can make a big difference.

The Servant Girl's Discussion Guide

And the Syrians had gone out by companies, and had brought away captive out of the land of Israel a little maid; and she waited on Naaman's wife. (2 KINGS 5:2)

As the servant girl leaves to go back into the stands, we realize our time with her was too short. Our mind is flooded with questions we want to ask her. This discussion section gives us an opportunity to study the servant girl's message and reflect on what we have learned from her.

QUESTION FOR THE SERVANT GIRL: Were you surprised that God would use you? ______________

____

____

QUESTION FOR PERSONAL REFLECTION: When have you been surprised that God has used you? How many other "no-names" can you think of that God has worked through? ____________________

____

____

QUESTION FOR THE SERVANT GIRL: Where did you find the boldness to speak to this important man?

____

____

____

QUESTION FOR PERSONAL REFLECTION: Are there some people that you are hesitant to share your faith with? ____________________

____

____

QUESTION FOR THE SERVANT GIRL: Where did you develop your strong beliefs? ____________

____

____

QUESTION FOR PERSONAL REFLECTION: Do your beliefs and values stand out in different environments? ____________________________

____

____

QUESTION FOR THE SERVANT GIRL: Why would such an important man listen to you? ____________

____

____

QUESTION FOR PERSONAL REFLECTION: What is credible about your life that would make other people listen to you? Are there areas in which you lack credibility? If so, how does this limit your influence with others? ______________________

____

____

QUESTION FOR THE SERVANT GIRL: How did you feel when the Captain came home healed? ___________

____

____

QUESTION FOR PERSONAL REFLECTION: Who was the last person you helped through your own efforts? How did you feel knowing you had helped him or her? ____

____

____

David

You Can Overcome the Limitations Others Put on You

David, perhaps more than anyone else in the stadium, is the person I most want to run a lap with. I watch him as he approaches us. He is dressed as a king in colorful robes with a jeweled sword on his hip and a crown on his head, but carries himself like a great warrior—powerful, relaxed yet alert, and poised for any situation.

I wonder what the greatest king of Israel will say to us. Will he talk about the successful battles he led? Will he share the loneliness he felt as he hid from King Saul? Maybe he will tell us how he expanded Israel's territory, or how he felt when he wrote the psalms. He is a man after God's own heart, so any words that fall from his lips will be like pearls.

As he gets closer, we can see that he has the eyes of a man who has seen much—pain, grief, and death—yet he doesn't look bitter or hard. His countenance is open. He comes alongside us, running easily. And then this champion of champions and king of kings says, "*You can overcome the limitations others put on you.*"

What Potential?

When we think of David, we don't immediately think of limitations. Here is a man who achieved great success and made it to the top. He was a great warrior and the greatest of kings. Yet there were many who never saw his potential. As a young man, he didn't look like a warrior or a king. He was the youngest in his family, and as a boy he did not receive affirmation from those around him.

David's greatest battles in his early years were not against the bear or the lion he slew while protecting his father's sheep. His greatest obstacles were created by the people who tried to put limitations on him. Look at how others saw and treated David:

Jesse Did Not Think David Had King-Potential

Are you someone who feels the pain of having a parent not believe in you? David knew that pain. David's father, Jesse, became very excited when he learned that the prophet Samuel was coming to anoint one of his sons to be Israel's next king. He must have talked to his wife for hours, considering the fine qualities each son possessed. They probably couldn't sleep that night for thinking about it. *Which son will God choose?* they wondered.

When Samuel arrived at Jesse's house to anoint one of the boys, Jesse lined up the ones he thought had king-potential. That was every son—*except* David. Jesse didn't even bother to call David in from the fields. And at first, the prophet thought the way Jesse did. He judged the sons based on who looked like a king. But God had something else in mind. Scripture states:

> He looked at [Jesse's eldest son] Eliab and said, "Surely the LORD's anointed is before Him!" But the LORD said to Samuel, "Do not look at his appearance or at his physical stature, because I have refused him. For the LORD does not see as man sees; for man looks at the outward appearance, but the LORD looks at the heart." (1 SAM. 16:6-7)

Jesse paraded seven sons before Samuel, yet God didn't choose any of them. God wanted David, the one with heart. Isn't it reassuring to know that God values us for who we truly are, even if our family doesn't?

David's Brothers Did Not Think He Had Warrior-Potential

David experienced similar rejection from his brothers. When Israel was at war with the Philistines, three of David's brothers became soldiers in Israel's army. David was left at home to care for his father's flocks. And when Jesse did send David down to the battle lines to take his brothers food and to bring back news, his brothers abused him—

especially when David expressed interest in doing battle with Goliath when all the soldiers feared him. The Bible says his brother Eliab became angry and said, "Why did you come down here? And with whom have you left those few sheep in the wilderness? I know your pride and the insolence of your heart, for you have come down to see the battle" (1 Sam. 17:28). His brothers saw him as nothing more than an errand boy, but he was really a man with a mission.

King Saul Did Not Think David Had Champion-Potential

When King Saul heard that there was someone in the camp who was willing to fight Goliath, he sent for him. He was no doubt expecting a grizzled veteran to face the nine-feet-nine-inch-tall Philistine warrior. Who walked in but a shepherd boy, saying, "Let no man's heart fail because of him; your servant will go and fight with this Philistine."

Saul's response reveals his skepticism. He said to David, "You are not able to go against this Philistine to fight with him; for you are a youth, and he a man of war from his youth" (1 Sam.

17:32-33). Saul thought David wasn't champion material, that he wasn't up for the task. To make up for what the king perceived to be David's shortcomings, Saul tried to get David to wear his royal armor. (Why not—Saul wasn't using it for anything!) But of course, the armor of a tall, mature warrior like Saul wouldn't fit a boy like David, and he took it off. David didn't allow Saul to hinder him with his low expectations or his bulky armor. He went out to face Goliath just as he was.

Goliath Did Not Think David Had Even Opponent-Potential

The final insult for David came when Goliath saw him advancing to meet him in battle. The huge Philistine took one look at the shepherd boy and reacted negatively. Scripture says,

> So the Philistine said to David, "Am I a dog, that you come to me with sticks?" And the Philistine cursed David by his gods. And the Philistine said to David, "Come to me, and I will give your

> flesh to the birds of the air and the beasts of the field!" (1 SAM. 17:43-44)

Goliath despised David and believed that the boy wasn't even worthy of a proper burial, and with those words, he attacked him.

You can easily determine the caliber of a person by the amount of opposition it takes to discourage him or her. David faced great opposition. Everyone told David he had no potential, but he was able to:

- go beyond his family (relational limitations)
- go beyond the "King Sauls" (leadership limitations)
- go beyond the "Goliaths" (skill limitations)

He threw off all the limitations that others placed on him and he killed Goliath. And when he did, he removed the limitations from the army of Israel and they routed the Philistine army. His personal victory turned into a victory for the entire nation!

David's Words of Encouragement

As we round the track, I think about the boy that David was, and how even he—a man after God's own heart who grew up to be a great king—had to start out with nothing but hope and potential. I am quickly snapped out of these reflective thoughts by David's desire to share these final words of encouragement with us:

- "*Limitations don't limit us unless we let them.* My father, my brothers, and my leader all thought I had no potential. But in reality, I had the greatest potential of all; I had God-potential. When I was young I was able to keep growing in spite of the negative reactions of others because of God's assistance. I never forgot the day Samuel anointed me. From that day on the Spirit of the Lord came upon me in power. And I realized that God could strengthen me to rise above limitations that life and others would try to place on me. My friend, He can also do that for you!"
- "*Don't try to be someone else when others impose limitations on you.* When Saul realized I

was going to fight Goliath, he tried to put his armor on me. He wanted me to attack the problem as he would. I tried the armor on because he intimidated me, but of course it didn't fit. At that moment, I realized that God didn't want a substitute Saul; He wanted me! God will never hold you accountable for gifts you don't have or responsibilities He hasn't given you. He wants you to be yourself!"

◆ *"When you rise above your limitations, you can help others do the same.* The day I faced Goliath, I thought only of defeating him. I never realized that my victory would become Israel's victory. The moment Goliath fell, the army of Israel rose. Their fear and intimidation were replaced by courage and aggressiveness. That day I learned my greatest leadership lesson: People follow the example of their leader. The moment that I accomplished more than anyone thought was possible . . . so did my people!"

David's Prayer for Us

Lord God,

Help my friends to see themselves as You see them, not as others do, to focus on what can be accomplished with You and not what can't be accomplished without You, and to rise above the limitations placed on them by others, so that they might help others rise above their limitations.

Amen

As David finishes praying, I wonder to myself, *Is there anyone who can encourage and empower me more than the nine people who have taken time to run a lap with me? Certainly I have run with and listened to the best of the best!* I thank David for his prayer, and he says one last thing to us before he goes: "I know you will be encouraged by the last person who will run with you because he, more than any other person in my life, encouraged me. That person, of course, is Jonathan!"

David's Discussion Guide

Then said David to the Philistine, Thou comest to me with a sword, and with a spear, and with a shield: but I come to thee in the name of the LORD of hosts, the God of the armies of Israel, whom thou hast defied. (1 SAMUEL 17:45)

As David leaves to go back into the stands, we realize our time with him was too short. Our mind is flooded with questions we want to ask him. This discussion section gives us an opportunity to study David's message and reflect on what we have learned from him.

QUESTION FOR DAVID: How did you overcome the limitations your family placed on you?

___

___

QUESTION FOR PERSONAL REFLECTION: What limitations have others placed upon me? Am I overcoming them? If so, how? ____________________

____

____

QUESTION FOR DAVID: Where did you learn to trust in God instead of Saul's armor? ____________

____

____

QUESTION FOR PERSONAL REFLECTION: When I face a challenge do I rely on my faith or do I rely on my abilities? ______________________________

____

____

QUESTION FOR DAVID: Did the anointing of Samuel at Jesse's house provide a breakthrough for you? Were you different from that day on? __________

____

____

QUESTION FOR PERSONAL REFLECTION: What breakthrough have I experienced in my life that enabled me to live on a higher level? ____________________

____

____

QUESTION FOR DAVID: Did you realize that your victories would bring victories to others? __________

____

____

QUESTION FOR PERSONAL REFLECTION: Can I point to times where my breakthroughs in life enabled others to experience success? ____________________

____

____

QUESTION FOR DAVID: For many years you had to patiently wait to become King of Israel. Was that difficult? ______________________________

____

____

QUESTION FOR PERSONAL REFLECTION: How patient am I waiting for something God has promised me?

____

____

____

Jonathan

Strengthen a Leader and Save a Nation

David leaves us and moves back toward the stands. In the place where all the other giants of the faith have passed one another, David stops for a moment and grabs Jonathan in a hearty embrace. Then David disappears into the stands and Jonathan comes out to greet us. We have just spent time with the greatest of Israel's kings. Now we will be running with the king-maker.

"My friends," Jonathan says, "you live in an age when winning at all costs and looking out for number one are exalted as virtues. The words of the Proverbs writer could have been penned today: 'Most men will proclaim each his own goodness, but who can find a faithful man?' (20:6). People seem to have forgotten what it means to serve others or exhibit true loyalty. In such a time as this, what I will tell you becomes doubly important: *Strengthen a leader and save a nation."*

Jonathan has credibility like no one else in the Bible to deliver such a message. While other people in David's life were trying to keep him down by putting limitations on him, Jonathan did the opposite. He lifted David up and strengthened him so that he could meet his trials and beat his oppressors.

Friends for Life

The two men became fast friends soon after David killed Goliath. Scripture says:

> Now when he had finished speaking to Saul, the soul of Jonathan was knit to the soul of

> David, and Jonathan loved him as his own soul. Saul took him that day, and would not let him go home to his father's house anymore. Then Jonathan and David made a covenant, because he loved him as his own soul. And Jonathan took off the robe that was on him and gave it to David, with his armor, even to his sword and his bow and his belt." (1 SAM. 18:1-4)

From that point on, Jonathan was willing to do anything to help David, and that was good because David would need a lot of help.

◆ *David was taken out of his comfort zone.* The day David killed Goliath *everything* changed in his life. He went from unknown boy to hero and from shepherd to leader.

◆ *King Saul was jealous of David and constantly tried to destroy him.* The king was furious when the people sang, "Saul has slain his thousands, and David his tens of thousands."

◆ *David's life was an emotional roller coaster.* One moment David was leading the army of Israel and the next moment he was hiding from the same army because Saul was deploying it to try to kill him.

◆ *David faced many severe challenges.* David was often in over his head. His assignments from the king were difficult and the expectations of the people were high. Without help, he would not survive.

So at every turn, Jonathan helped David. And that is what made all the difference for David, the nation, and the people.

Big-Picture Power

What empowered Jonathan to put David ahead of himself and serve him? After all, Jonathan was the prince of Israel and the rightful heir to the throne. But from the moment he first met David, Jonathan understood David's potential (unlike King Saul, David's brothers, or even David's father). Jonathan saw the big picture.

Jonathan's Big-Picture Thinking Allowed Him to See Himself from the Right Perspective

The first great advantage of seeing the big picture is being able to judge yourself realistically. If you *overestimate* your value, you may do things just to feed your ego. If you *underestimate* your value, you may become discouraged and neglect doing the things you *can* do. But the big picture gives you a right picture of yourself. When Jonathan saw David after he killed Goliath, the prince realized that David had the potential to be a better leader than his father or himself. And Jonathan realized that he was no longer the best person to ascend to the throne.

Jonathan's Big-Picture Thinking Allowed Him to See Others from the Right Perspective

When Jonathan saw himself realistically, he was free to treat others as they deserved. That meant preserving David's life and serving him. Jonathan knew that helping David would benefit the kingdom more than promoting himself as Israel's future ruler. And while King Saul, his father, continually tried to manipulate situations to eliminate David as a threat to him, Jonathan worked hard to help his friend. He strategically invested his time and energy for David's success.

Jonathan's Big-Picture Thinking Allowed Him to Do What's Right from God's Perspective

Often our personal ambition clouds God's direction for our lives. But Jonathan's grasp of the big picture helped him to understand what God desired. Even though it didn't benefit him personally, Jonathan obeyed God and didn't whine about his rights. Jonathan gave up his own future on the throne to serve the rightful person who would take it. The result? The reign of David was the greatest in Israel's history. Because he was so deeply committed to David's future, Jonathan ended up saving the entire nation of Israel from destruction.

Jonathan's Words of Encouragement

Before I know it, our lap is nearly finished. As we approach the final turn in the track, Jonathan says:

◆ *"Only when you see what is important will you be willing to do the seemingly unimportant.* I did not serve David because I lacked potential. I served him because he had greater potential. As I look back on my life, my greatest joy was helping David succeed to the throne. Remember, it takes a lot of king-makers to make a king!"

◆ *"Every time you encounter people with potential, you must make a choice.* You can either hurt them or help them. My father chose to hurt David. What would have happened if my dad had helped David? The king's time would have been spent on productive instead of destructive things. The kingdom would have been united instead of divided. My relationship with my father would have been greatly improved. And God's blessings would have continued on my father's leadership. A legacy of leadership would have been passed down to David. Sadly, in the end, my father did not hurt David; he hurt himself."

◆ *"As a supporter, you share in your leader's success.* When you help a leader, you share in whatever he or she achieves. As I helped my friend

David, I knew that I was serving God, and whatever benefits the nation of Israel received came about in part through my efforts. The same is true for you. You don't have to be on the front lines to share in the rewards or to make a great impact. Strengthen your leader, and you can help save your nation."

Jonathan's Prayer for Us

Sovereign Master and King,

Please empower my friends to see the big picture so they may know their place and be glad to be a part of something great, cultivate the right attitude toward the potential and success of others, and possess a servant's heart that receives great joy in adding value to leaders.

Amen

I am encouraged by Jonathan's words. From my own experience in teaching leadership, I know that people often think leaders are self-sufficient. But if anything, my work with leaders has taught me that the greatest need in a leader's life is to have a Jonathan beside him or her.

As we come to the end of the track, Jonathan stops us for a moment. And we notice that all the people in the stands—thousands upon thousands of them—are on their feet. And they are clapping and cheering for you and me. The thunderous roar is electrifying! "Now," says Jonathan, "I am about to go back and take my place with the others. It has been our hearts' desire to encourage and empower you. When you grow weary, think of us. When you fall down, get up, knowing that we are cheering for you. And every time you experience a victory, know that everyone in heaven is rejoicing with you.

"But there is one thing more I must tell you," he says. "You need not wait until you're sitting among us to cheer on your fellow runners. Empower others as you meet them along the way. Pick them up when they fall, help them to run better, and pass along what we have taught you. And run with endurance the race that is set before you, looking at Jesus, the author and finisher of our faith, lest you become weary and discouraged in your souls."

With that, Jonathan climbs up into the stands

and takes his place beside David. For a few moments, we just soak in the scene and listen to the roar of encouragement. And then we know it's our time to run. With the cheers still ringing in our ears, we leave the stadium, better equipped to keep running for another day.

Jonathan's Discussion Guide

Then Jonathan and David made a covenant, because he loved him as his own soul. And Jonathan stripped himself of the robe that was upon him, and gave it to David, and his garments, even to his sword, and to his bow, and to his girdle. (1 SAMUEL 18:3-4)

As Jonathan leaves to go back into the stands, we realize our time with him was too short. Our mind is flooded with questions we want to ask him. This discussion section gives us an opportunity to study Jonathan's message and reflect on what we have learned from him.

QUESTION FOR JONATHAN: When did you see David's potential and decide to become his faithful friend? ________________________________

____

____

QUESTION FOR PERSONAL REFLECTION: Do I see the potential in others? ______________________

____

____

QUESTION FOR JONATHAN: Was it difficult giving up your rights as a future king to serve David?

____

____

____

QUESTION FOR PERSONAL REFLECTION: Do I often give up my rights to serve others? Are there times when this is difficult? ____________________

____

____

QUESTION FOR JONATHAN: You realized that David's potential for leadership was greater than yours. Was that difficult to assess? ________________

____

____

QUESTION FOR PERSONAL REFLECTION: Do I realistically see myself and others? When someone is more gifted than me, how do I feel toward them? Do I enjoy serving them? ________________

____

____

QUESTION FOR JONATHAN: How difficult was it to be in the middle between your father Saul and David? How did you make the decision to support David?

____

____

____

QUESTION FOR PERSONAL REFLECTION: Am I often placed between friends and family? How do I deal with this situation? ______________________

QUESTION FOR JONATHAN: David was the greatest king in Israel. Did you feel a part of his success?

QUESTION FOR PERSONAL REFLECTION: When I help others and they succeed, do I feel a part of that success? Do I rejoice with them? Am I lifting someone to a higher level? ______________________

Learn More about the Giants of the Faith

To learn more about the biblical leaders contained in *Running with the Giants,* read the following passages from the Bible:

THE HALL OF FAITH PASSAGE
HEBREWS 11:1-40

NOAH
GENESIS 6:1–10:32

ESTHER
ESTHER 1:1–10:3

JOSEPH
GENESIS 35:16-26 and 37:1–50:26

MOSES
EXODUS 1:1 through DEUTERONOMY 34:12

REBEKAH

GENESIS 24:1-67

ABRAHAM

GENESIS 11:27–25:11

NEHEMIAH

NEHEMIAH 1:1–13:31

THE SERVANT GIRL

2 KINGS 5:1-27

DAVID

1 SAMUEL 16:1-1, KINGS 2:12, and
1 CHRONICLES 11:1–29:30

JONATHAN

1 SAMUEL 14:1-46, 20:1-42, and 31:1-13

About the Author

Dr. John C. Maxwell is the author of three *New York Times* bestsellers on the subject of leadership: *The 21 Irrefutable Laws of Leadership, Failing Forward,* and *Developing the Leader Within You.* Other books include *The 17 Indisputable Laws of Teamwork, The 21 Indispensable Qualities of a Leader, The 21 Most Powerful Minutes in a Leader's Day,* and *Success One Day at a Time.*

Dr. Maxwell is also a popular speaker for corporations such as AFLAC, Salem Communications, Wal-Mart, and Books-a-Million and each year speaks to more than 350,000 people. He has appeared as a guest on *Good Morning, America.* He is the founder of The INJOY Group in Atlanta, Georgia.

Dr. Maxwell received his doctorate from Fuller Theological Seminary. He lives with his wife in Atlanta.

It's easy to begin a training regimen, but it's hard to stay with the program. INJOY® understands that side of human nature and we want to do what we can to help you continue your growth. Prepare to take the next step toward *Running with the Giants!*

Log on to **RunningwiththeGiants.com** and receive a free copy of *Biblical Images of Leadership.* This lesson was specifically chosen from John C. Maxwell's INJOY Life Club series to help you take the next step in your training program!

Biblical Images of Leadership is available to you either online in streaming audio format or if you would prefer to add this lesson to your personal training library, we can ship you a copy on either audiocassette or CD for a minimal shipping charge of $2.00.

Visit the author at www.RunningwiththeGiants.com and download your FREE audio lesson! Available online or on audiocassette/CD.